ALL EMPTY VESSELS

Aaron Kent is a working-class writer, stroke survivor, and insomniac from Cornwall. His 2nd collection, *The Working Classic*, is available from the87press. He has read his poetry for The BBC, The Shakespeare Birthplace Trust, and Stroke Association, had work published in various journals, and is an Arvon tutor. His poetry has been translated into languages including French, Hungarian, German, Cymraeg, and Kernewek, and has been set to music.

Stuart McPherson is a prize-winning poet from the UK. His poems have appeared in *Butcher's Dog Magazine*, *Bath Magg*, *Poetry Wales*, *Anthropocene*, *Blackbox Manifold*, *Prelude* and *One Hand Clapping*. In October 2022, Stuart was the winner of the Ambit Annual Poetry Competition. His second collection, *End Ceremonies*, was published via Broken Sleep Books on August 31st 2023.

Also by Aaron Kent

The Working Classic	(the87press, 2023)
The Rise Of...	(Broken Sleep Books, 2022)
Angels the Size of Houses	(Shearsman, 2021)
The Last Hundred	(Guillemot, 2020)

Also by Stuart McPherson

End Ceremonies	(Broken Sleep Books, 2023)
Obligate Carnivore	(Broken Sleep Books, 2022)
Waterbearer	(Broken Sleep Books, 2021)
Pale Mnemonic	(Legitimate Snack, 2021)

PRAISE for *All Empty Vessels*

Aaron Kent and Stuart McPherson's *All Empty Vessels* is a multi-person conversation. Two men in conversation with imagination, language, illness, power and limitation. Back and forth, between the poets — whose friendship is evident in the collaboration — the reader is brought into the intimate space of confession, creativity, chaos and collaboration. This joint collection makes few promises, but the one it demonstrates is that even in emptiness, connection is a companion for *All Empty Vessels*.
— Pádraig Ó Tuama

This diurnal/nocturnal double act spits and wheezes an electro-magnetic sociology of the underdog spirit with venom and flare. Animated by a summonings or invocation of Edgar Allan Poe and a character named 'Poet', the reader is razed by a wild-card graffiti of the spirit. This is a Butoh of working class robustness/consciousness: a dance of death performed to the British class system, executed on an altar of flickering screens, night walks, radiophonic dead air and luminous introspection. A haunting is bad enough, but a double haunting, where Kent summons McPherson and McPherson responds to Kent, reads like a vigorous card game: the flickering deck of their contaminant thought laid down swiftly, card by card, and without remorse. And yet, there is bathos, tenderness and liminality. In a dual showmanship of a new warning for both past and future, these are 'new forgeries. . . for invisible dawns' housed in a 'coffin rolled across a minefield'. You stand warned.
— MacGillivray

Two poets writing so brilliantly and wearing a full suit of artistic armoury; what's not to like? Aaron Kent and Stuart McPherson's poetics are simultaneously interfused and complimentary of one another, befitting a book of exceptionally nuanced, collaborative poems and texts. Open, ludic, tender, defiant and with multiple helpings of satiric wit, nothing appears off limits in these poems of lyric intimacy, cast across psychological (and socio-political) time and space. Kent and McPherson are a pair of shapeshifters, metamorphic, restless, and so continually uncovering and recovering perceptions within a spindled self. Here, hearts become mirrors in a family tree, the 'I' orbits 'delicately as a torpedo on payday' and desire is haunted 'with the eyes of a gundog'. Death is cast too, never far away like an eye at the porthole. This metamorphic effect tilts the poem from sea to sky and back down to earth again, ensuring the writing is located at all times, bound by both poet's perfect-pitch musicianship. *All Empty Vessels* listens in to the overboiling temperature of the times. This is a bicameral poetics that comes with stark and subtle warnings. Poets too are implicated, everything is at stake—it's all or nothing, as Jean Genet said it must be. Time to wake up from 'tone-deaf banjo' playing and 'ceremonial bootlicking', or else 'the future watches rabbits thrashing in the snares'. Read this and be fully nourished, yet hungry and, as I did, read it all over again.
— James Byrne

All Empty Vessels

Aaron Kent
&
Stuart McPherson

Broken Sleep Books

© 2023 Aaron Kent & Stuart McPherson All rights reserved; no part of this book may be reproduced by any means without the publisher's permission.

ISBN: 978-1-916938-19-9

The author has asserted their right to be identified as the author of this Work in accordance with the Copyright, Designs and Patents Act 1988

Cover designed by Aaron Kent & Stuart McPherson

Edited and Typeset by Aaron Kent

Broken Sleep Books Ltd	Broken Sleep Books Ltd
Rhydwen	Fair View
Talgarreg	St Georges Road
Ceredigion	Cornwall
SA44 4HB	PL26 7YH

Contents

EDGAR

I	13
II	14
III	15
IV	16
V	17
VI	18

FAMILY MATTERS

THE VILLAGE ACRES	21
CLUTCH	22
A HEART IN THE BRANCHES OF A FAMILY TREE	23
UNKNOWN SOLDIER	24
SIMILAR DAYS TO THIS	25
MILKY BUTTON	26

MOONMARINE

TRAINING WEREWOLVES	29
ON CLIMBING LOW IN WITNESS	30
SOUL, PLEXUS	31
PERIGEE	32
OCELOT NEBULA	33
AS THE LIGHTS BLINK OUT AND THE SOUL BLEEDS ITSELF HOLLOW	34

DESTROY ALL POETRY

POET MAKES A FRIEND	37
POET INSALUBRIOUS	38
POET MISTAKEN FOR BIG BANG	39
POET'S SECRET	40
POET SUBMITS	41
POET'S UNDOING	42

SWITCH

IMPOSSIBLE WINTERSLEEP	45
PRAISE BE THE OCEAN, AND MYRIAD REASONS TO DROWN IN IT	47
MUSIC FOR A COLD SNAP	48

EIGHTY FIVE PERCENT MORTALITY RATE	49
RENT-A-PRICK	50
BURIAL RITES FOR DISTANT BOATS	51

NIGHT SONNETS

NIGHT SONNET #1	55
NIGHT SONNET #2	56
NIGHT SONNET #3	57
NIGHT SONNET #4	58
NIGHT SONNET #5	59
NIGHT SONNET #6	60

ANTI-CAPITALIST, ANTI-BASTARD

THAT ALL OF THIS COULD BE ERASED	63
TINY THINGS, LIKE AN EGO BURSTING	64
LANDING OUTSIDE WATER	65
INTRODUCTION TO COMPULSORY SEA SHANTIES	66
A COLLECTIVE NOUN IS A HOSTILE STATE	67
A RECORDED CONVERSATION WITH AN AWARD-WINNING AUTHOR	68

FRAILTY

IN THE DUSK OF OUR POST-HONEYMOON ERA	71
CLEAR AIR	72
ELEPHANT CIRCA 1989	73
SOMEONE LEFT THE DOOR OPEN IN THE WAR ROOM	74
WE ARE STILL HERE DESPITE EVERYTHING	75
DEFICIT	76

DARLING LET ME DIE IN PEACE

AN OBITUARY	79
FIRE-STARTER	80
INCOMPATIBLE AT BEST	81
A COLLECTION OF DRAMATIC MONOLOGUES ON THE BIG SCREEN	82
POSSUM, DROWNING	83
EVENTIDE PRAYER FOR A BASTARD CAPITALIST	84

POST-BREXIT WORKER BLUES

AT THE END OF IT ALL	87
IF ONLY	88
SO MANY MEN, SO QUIET THE TOWNS	91
TRUE STORY	92
FROM DISPATCII TO SUBURBIA	93
GREAT BRITAIN	94

ALL ENGLISH WANK

ONCE MORE WITH A BODY COUNT	97
TWO TRUTHS AND A LIE, BUT THEY'RE ALL TRUE	98
SORRY, MY LOVE	99
WHILE POPPING THE FILM ON A READY MEAL I CONSIDER TURNING THE KNIFE ON MYSELF	100
CROMULENT CREAMPIE	101
LAZARUS' LEFT BOLLOCK	102

ADOLESENCE IS A BITTER PILL SWALLOWED TWICE

NOT ALL TEENAGE BEDROOMS ARE THE SAME.	105
ADOLESCENT NOSTALGIA IS NEVER A ONE TRICK PONY	106
OVERDRAMATIC HALLOWEEN SEX POEM	107
THE PUNK'S PICNIC WAS INSANE	110
WITHOUT FAILSAFES	111
RELIEF	112

EPHEMERAL MATERIAL INCIDENT

TO DISAPPEAR. TO FALL ASLEEP	115

MISSION ANALYSES: RHODEDENDRON

A KAPUŐRÖK MEGSZŰNÉSE / HERLIN-BAMLET PART II	119

EDGAR

by Aaron Kent

Ah, distinctly I remember it was in the bleak December;
And each separate dying ember wrought its ghost upon the floor.

— Edgar Allen Poe, 'The Raven'

I

Gentle or not, you lost me at Raven. Every time a bird's beak acts as a doorbell, a librarian shreds a book on Avian Flu. Lenore never loved you enough to be Virginia, barely enough to not confuse you with a racing pigeon. Edgar, I've been dreaming I'm you again, dreaming of our poor soul fed to a petting zoo where the children confuse crows for magpies, confuse trinkets for enough gold to buy a house and set our family up for life. We've earned the wrath of birds and poetry won't save us; birds don't care for sonnets. The man on the moon is stabbing himself nightly, inflicting tiny cuts so when the knife storm arrives he may be immune. Write about that, Edgar, write about that in your syphilitic state. Nobody remembers your final words but I can hazard a guess; eyes bent to the heavens, back arched in the drunken throes of a life seeping away, did you call out for an albatross? Did you see the blood pool on the moon's craters, hear a heart beating somewhere three houses over, and wish you'd picked a puffin to bother you?

II

I haven't been myself lately
so forgive me if I sound a little strange,
I've chosen to bury my body under the porch.
You know what that's like, Edgar,
to live a life under floorboards,
to dream of rising damp.
At the edge of the soil
where light and sound never meet,
I hope to understand the value of silence.
I miss my hands on my cheeks,
my hands over my mouth
my hands around my neck.
O, to lie here, on the precipice
of somewhere else, awaiting
the slender sleep of sirens.

III

I am at the end of my rope,
waiting for any kind of release
from this small-minded town
you never liked
but tolerated.
I've been writing you letters, but I hear
the wind's a rascal
with a penchant for mischief.
These poems are so slow, Edgar,
and so I think I'm done.
O, I miss you,
you've always been good to me,
even when I was evil,
when I was the devil,
not that the devil ever loved you.
But Edgar, I never liked myself.
You do yourself more than enough justice.
I couldn't bear to be alone,
so I'm waiting for a little rain,
a little breeze,
a little death.
I have already tried to die
in this city
and failed to be beautiful
or clever.

IV

I am on the verge of living and all I ask is for you to keep these last words of mine before they are eaten up by time, burnt, dissolved, buried beneath the terrain. How to get you to understand, Edgar, how to get you to understand is my question. Is it a matter of being born to do so? Or is it a matter of losing yourself so you can live? I don't know, Edgar, I just want to touch you and have you touch me. This is a thing, Edgar, that may take forever to learn how to do. It's an endless game of chicken in the dark where neither of us is sure who's the driver and who's the mark waiting for the split second. We're both on our knees but only I have the power to make it stop. I am on the verge of living, you are on the verge of death, Edgar. A man of action I tell myself; a man of inaction I tell myself. I'll never get what I want unless you give it to me.

V

I'm not done
    with you yet,
not done
    with you yet,
but I'm sick
    of this
        damned city,
and I want to
    die
        again.
I've made it through
        difficult times,
the night of
    my grandfather's funeral,
but it's different
    this time,
the way the wind
        blows
            harder.
I want to die,
    Edgar.
I want to die.

VI

I remember you had an appointment with the dentist the night you called to tell me you were quitting drinking. No, that's not right, my eyes weren't red, and I was wearing a white dress with black shoes. You were trying to quit drinking, and I lost the words you said to me. How did they go? I can't remember. I know I asked you if I should get a vasectomy. How's it that I remember the conversation so clearly but you don't remember calling me? I remember that I didn't want a child, not with you and I do remember telling you that. I have children. I've had children for a long time. No, my eyes *were* red and I *wasn't* wearing a dress. Was it that night I said to you *tell me you love me before you go to sleep* and you said *I don't love you*. How can you live with that, Edgar? How can you sleep knowing that you've only loved two people in your life, and both of them were you? You have an appointment with your dentist, Edgar, and you're still afraid of a pain that won't end. You walk up the stairs, Edgar, but you don't go inside. You're afraid. Tell me you've quit, Edgar. You've quit, right? Tell me you have. Tell me you have quit, Edgar, so I can say to you *go home, you have quit.*

FAMILY MATTERS

by Stuart McPherson

We sit down in the smell of the past and rise in a light that is already leaving.
— Rita Dove, 'November for Beginners'

THE VILLAGE ACRES

When I think about you, father,
I think about the field where we shot
those rats with a walnut stocked gun.

The spark of metal pellets off a dusty
stable floor. Yellow cloud, yellow front teeth,
a curl of dark red from a gurning mouth.

To somehow be at peace, this quick knotting
up of flesh. Yellow as the honeybees bunched
above your shirt as you ran down the acre.

Young birch tree planted in the middle learning
to thrive in the immediacy of death. The chop of
a battered shovel saddened by your frown.

Stood in the brackish heat of a late summer sun,
I hear the shriek of insects wild under straw, watch
the shapes stooped in the dust of the poultry run.

This heavy world sloshing in a rusty pail carried at
arm's length, your misunderstanding displayed on
palms way too tentative to hold a child.

CLUTCH

Lost without map. No
coordinates nor shred of
smooth papery acetate.
North star shattered under
swung nub of metal minus
safety in the warm embrace
of underground lairs.
So much wonderment at what
might be, has been, *or is*.

When I think about the word
needs I am sunken in the
desert sand, palm trees leaning
in, angular, scarce. Each
slithering scale of snake is a long
tooth in the leg. Every mirage
destitute of cool moisture
oppositional to a desperate
flicking tongue.

At the table your outline feasts
on soft oblong eggs; rubbery,
pliable. Cold blood runs from
head to tail wrapped around
the imprint of a young crescent,
too slow, too unsure of becoming
unwound from the burrow into
a world never felt with any
degree of confidence.

A HEART IN THE BRANCHES OF A FAMILY TREE

Mirror.
Ill- hung and
smudged by hand.

Wiped clean as
though absolved, ignored by
reflections of the singing self.

I know you, it says. *We know
how well you walk*, it mutters
under burgeoning skies.

As if by magic it would
suck up all these imperfect
little pieces scattered in a

garnet hole, the one that
both our hands force open
from time to time.

UNKNOWN SOLDIER

Well dressed, less expression, but
walking from dining room to darkened
staircase. Upwards like a feather blown
from downy mattress, deflated, downcast
in its plumping sigh.

You *had* seen it, as had the paint-pocked
hairs on your muscular arms. Goose bumped
by day, to appear at night inside the kitchen,
the midpoint just before dawn and chorus as
jagged shard.

He marched right by musket on collarbone.
Write, you said, so insistent in tone, a rapid
signal scratched on the lip of an old envelope.
Old equations, a grey tip pencil chewed to
a woody pulp.

This sharing of words an infrequent closeness
sandwiched together in-between all botched
paternities, as floating figures stepping out
towards the money tree, as breath cut into leaf
and bluntly carved into flesh.

> *By unlit room, our duplicate notes.*
> *Is this the science of saying then,*
> *just how much you meant to me?*

SIMILAR DAYS TO THIS

From the kitchen, Frederick says that it's not
entirely his job to provide *all* sustenance, *all* provision
of warmth and tenderness. I sit in the stairwell
talking about comparison to others.
From the light of the terrace, the table is set with
brioche, hot chocolate, the echoes of bygone years.
A French holiday for him and her. For me, the crumbs
beneath the pantry door; a feast for a family of mice.
Why don't you ask your mother……?

Sliced ham bloodied pink, throbbing from the platter.
Above, the photos from New Orleans, the plane propeller,
caterpillars in the trees. Nothing is more cumbersome than
rage. As I sit amongst the furnishings of my own realm,
I see his shadow, the way they carried his coffin.
The flowers in my garden, pale roses, cabbages, carrots.
As does my shape, this familiar dragging backwards.

Desire: you haunt me with the eyes of a gundog,
its teeth set within a brace of torn, white sheets.

MILKY BUTTON

All I ever really wanted was
longevity & two caring bodies to
count on. To trust inside emergent
blue hours, be sheltered from the
rip of heavy tides. A harsh raking

across the cruellest latitudes even
in the knowledge of a rising sun,
each new moon made of gas & rock.
That maybe I wouldn't feel absence
as frigid as your refusal to wear

this cloak of August's healing light.
The chance to hold a body close as
family or exist in recurring nuclear
dreams imbued with hope, with fate,
the throb of accountability thrown

like paper cups so gently crushed.
Saltwater rolls the edge of a pale
milky button, *the places where we live*.
I am caught, never seeming able to
outrun the grip of all mutated love.

MOONMARINE

by Aaron Kent

———————

When the moon sails out / the bells fade into stillness
— Federico García Lorca, 'The Moon Wakes'

TRAINING WEREWOLVES

Under the illumination of
night's sterile propeller, the dark side
of this crescent depth gauge waxes lyrical
about submarines as nightmare fuel
for escape rooms. I wish to wane
slowly as an abandoned hatch, to orbit delicately
as a torpedo on payday, yet these
dreams reflect the ballast of a return I sacrificed
for an eclipse as seen from a bridge,
and the small grace of a weigthy periscope.
Bathe us as crew in the murky wilderness
of an ocean contemplating the formation of new
craters, and call us home when the time comes
to pacify sound and make mountains of moondust.

ON CLIMBING LOW IN WITNESS

To submerge a cloud is to navigate
among a bicycle's tremendous tendency
to sleep. Or so it feels watching us
patrol the ocean amid the guitaring
of periscopes. When I dive into the moon
I calculate the need to monitor for
stars at crush depth, the elephanting
of communications cut off by cameras
fathoms above the veneer of surface.
Maintaining a lie in a book is as simple
as manoeuvring the official secrets act
over pizza with friends. Every truth
is worth its own weight in silence.

SOUL, PLEXUS

There is a hole the size of a mechanic
in the side of the moon tonight,
and I both pity and love the engineer
who has so little sense as to
permit the snow to fall on its daft surface.
Every origami raindrop is an additional
shareholder for a much larger problem,
another story for a pint and a bag
of crisps split down the seam.
The timing chain has slipped, the cycle
is somehow ajar, and we are counting
Tarot cards, instead of days, until
the gentle death of everybody we know.

PERIGEE

One hydroplane into a myaterious slumber
and the cavitaion's snore brings us closer to
libration than liberation, allows the navigator
to rest for the entire lunation. Would you mind
if I sonar'd you dozing, recorded the regolith
of your propeller and snooze? Here we may
hammock in silver dreams and dive awake
in luminous catastrophe. I don't mind drifting
across weakened satellite phases and sea
states with you when you make hibernating
in craters bulkhead-secure. I am swoon and
faint on the seaway of a lunar eclipse. I am ready
to salvage the scream from the penumbra.

OCELOT NEBULA

We are desolate monoliths
to grotesque architects,
temples to forbidden
demigogues who percolate
gibbous above. In a slender
chromatic astral tube
we have learnt to build
selenic icons from garbage
prayers, like swerving
to avoid quasars and beacons.
There are whales the size
of celestial bodies among us,
and they plan on doing us harm.

AS THE LIGHTS BLINK OUT AND THE SOUL BLEEDS ITSELF HOLLOW

In any descent there is a moment where
the string slackens, the world loosens its
arches, and there sits, at the dawn of freefall,
a single cherry tree. The choice, then,
becomes not whether to eat or die,
but how many knots a tongue can wrap
itself in when bound by the laws of
gravity and engine failure. Humanity
dignifies these challenges with
dots and dashes, smoke signals
of thoughts and prayers, but in constant
downward motion, there remains no
need for communication besides
small utterances and mercy killings.

DESTROY ALL POETRY

by Stuart McPherson

And the flame fills all space, The demolition is total
— Ted Hughes, 'Notes for a Little Play

POET MAKES A FRIEND

In this house, in the deep stomach of it, the long neck
of distinct & uttered sound, *poet watched*, mulled on all earthy
conversation.

Latched on by hook, a shared sucking in of foggy breath, thin
as dawn around a scrag of old horse. *Poet plotted; poet paused.*

And *poet*, prising apart vulnerabilities of the mouth, climbed
inside by lanternlight, found a rose, fly flecked, all scrunched up,
petals curled like bleached skin. Coated. Pith ridden.

Bitter the face as it slipped its way past teeth, past the cape
of good hope, past the table emptied of fruit & all but rusting
nib of sword.

Poet entertained, poet asked. Poet stooped underneath a veiled
black box, immortalised in paper & shared, floating in the ether.

The sucking in of cheek & bone, a collapse of flesh underfoot.
The clambering up & over of shale, rattling rungs descended from
stepladders of the soul.

All was quiet. A sabre. A vampire bat in rafters. *Poet watched*,
washed both hands of musky peat, crumbled in the shallows.

POET INSALUBRIOUS

Poet in the backwash, the grimy whirlpool of a river
With the swollen moon
The rapture of the birds
The broken neck of man
The herding of the sheep
The splitting of a crow
The rubbing of the bread, garlic, tomatoes, salt
With the stomachs bloat
The red rage of a blunt horizon
The wilted crops above a shrew
The suspension of a dropping leaf
Everything constricted by worms, airless in the silt
The water thickens in its muddy slick
To choke the oil from its sump
Tattoo these calligraphies of Earth
Slop the houses with its tail
Hide the wreckage of the rancorous sky
And in its sludge, nothing mattered
Not in the eyes of God, nor his crumpled gatekeepers

POET MISTAKEN FOR BIG BANG

Poet sat serenely at the centre of the universe.
Observed the pale body as downward sloping.
Past erogenous zones so very eager for the
Creeping touch of *Poet*.

All orbiting gas and dust boiled in the seas of
Cerberus set deep in the Herculean groin.

Poet as magnanimous birth, galaxian entity.
Of all spiritual third eyes opening in the
Blinding white light of everything born
From *Poet*, cradled by *Poet* as creation.

Others, as in hair and skin, their thin nails formed
In infancies of written word, of naivety sculpted from
Blood and bone and mortar scraped deep into the
Cracks of a perfectly innocent nothingness.

Nothingness. A dove holding in its beak the twig of
Our souls knowing nothingness, tasting nothingness.

That nothing matters but the walking home of things.
A collective burial of all our lives, our brief successes,
Our rotten failures in the perpetual graves we hold
Within this shared state of being, of connected love.

And *Poet,* lost amongst the stars, the raging horses,
Holds aloft parchment as singular written oath.
Unatoned, and bathed in the midnight of ignorant sleep.

POET'S SECRET

Poet picked a flower.
A dotted wheel of Helianthus clicking at the nub.
   Loosened by fingertips, by desire.

They love me, they love me not.
The will to open third eyes *all seeing* as searchlight.
   Aching trees gathered by the liminal outcrop.

Of demise, of reparation scattered by fistfuls of
arcane teeth, pulped and bloody, rooted to the air.
   Nerve endings; a sharp tip of spear.

Poet scattered seeds, the magnolia, the ivory.
To leverage all things central to the world,
   Its gooey innards appearing keen.

Hidden there, the *I* of all storms. An incantation to
conjure all things barely hidden and deceived.
   Poet sang like crow; *of me! of me!*

The wind knowing all, fell to an eventual feather,
as did the nectaries, as did all organic matter
   heaped like tears by *poets* feet.

By the birches, the spidery oaks looking in. Nothing.
No one in the stone circle but shadowy shapes.
   And *poet*, once again all alone.

POET SUBMITS

Discontent with the shapeshifting of
    tricky words, or the suckling teats
from which all sustenance is garnered,
    Poet sent them out into the world.

Drifting leaves, the plasticity of a bag.
    The stagnation of a howling desert
plane, its littering of absence across
    all four corners of a lifeless globe.

On scabbed knees *Poet* bent below
    eternal sky, all false idols mirror
bound with smoke, a blunted nib of
    pen to flick upon the burning pyre.

Giddy *Poet,* eager hands blackened
    by ink squeezed from the sacks of
old squids too slippery to give up their
    secrets, scaled in unison of bloat.

'Why hold onto the knowledge of the
    deep?' asked *Poe*t, mad scribbling
under duress and choking the habitats
    of immortal pulped trees, unfussed.

'Listen' hissed the squid, as *Poet* drank
    down the viscous gloop, afraid of
not being seen, too distracted, a glut
    of beaks whispering, 'I told you so.'

POET'S UNDOING

Poet in the woods without trees.

Poet chops chops chops at the trunk.
Nothing falls but sheets of paper, a featherweight.
Poet is looking for the city, its bright lights for the
Paper to sit in, as living, as a breathing in.
*Poe*t sits for a while.
Ponders on the paper as flesh and blood.

Poet climbs the rock, stands upon its mossy top.
Poet sings, dances in the wind with the city
And in all its resplendent cacophony, sang back.
Poet hears a love song.
Poet steps on the bones of other*s*, runs towards
The silvering pool.

Poet sees the luminescence, hears the song of
The beating heart.
The lights shine, such luscious fruit, the pool
Reflects *poet*. *Poet* is the *only* poet and cannot taste
The rottenness, the mulching in the air.
Poet clutches paper, clutches at the hem.

In the city, poet severs arms and legs, plants both
Limbs upright as trees for all to bend towards.

Poet chops chops chops, chops chops chops

The woods are beautifully green, watered, plentiful

SWITCH

by Aaron Kent

You are barely even cold outside and six more miles of walking until I get to work.
— Dean Rhetoric, 'Cancer [+Pop Punk]'

IMPOSSIBLE WINTERSLEEP

If sleep doesn't catch me like a spider in a   glass
me and hope I stay dead   certain
every decision has our   best
foot forward. I've begun to   think
and I don't love it, I preferred the coma's hedonism.

Every portion of the human   brain
damage has left my life a   hated
waking up before sunrise, before I've had chance

to convince myself I'm   numb
-er one with a bullet. We're always so   sick
kickflip but can you backside tailslide?

I can't tune without breaking a guitar   string
up the fairy lights in   narrow
boat to live in. Every pig is looking for an excuse to   arrest
the hearts sudden stop. All of our and all of their and our.

This is mere seasonal reproach to clean the   drain
out and away with temporal floods   poured
downpour, and upwind. Frost   bitten
me again, he's just learning, but he laughed about time slipping

when I'm high, us crying out for a cliff to start   crumbling
biscuits to make a mess. Every   night
sleep tight, hold on to a near   miss
you dearly. There are   hundreds
and thousands if you're hungry,   out
-landish claims of a possum and a drunk escapade with mice.

I rest when I wander amongst the dying ivy   gripped
the bunk as the submarine left. That   smell
me where I've splashed aftershave,   snaked
me once but never again. This is the   first
time lucky with no second chances.

PRAISE BE THE OCEAN, AND MYRIAD REASONS TO DROWN IN IT

Floating requires more
than a little trust   fund
raising money for
some new leisure   centre
on the political spectrum
is a grift for exit   poll
tax and still counting
her dead piled in the   street
smart, sure, but I've got
absolutely no common   sense
is tingling, so get it checked
out for carbon   monoxide
kill for a shot at the man
who assassinated my mum.

MUSIC FOR A COLD SNAP

I have kept every coma on my   person
of interest to you, this headache, that   cough
up blood once more and I'm phoning for

the talking clock. This body is a   place
the tablets down and step away, let's   settle
down for a long hibernation. I am   better
not forget to leave the tap dripping, bones numb

from the cold snap of branches heaving a dry   laugh
track on American sitcoms. The clothes frozen on the   line
up for inspection, I still dream of my boots polished,

my bed made, my oppo face down on the   ground
coffee in the morning, vapourised dope at twilight,

a warrant officer shushing the room   choking
the throttle, counting miseries in memoirs.

EIGHTY FIVE PERCENT MORTALITY RATE

Heavy on the head, light on the ambivalence of dreams
since they took a scar of me, processed the   shape
up and breathe through your frontal lobe, this takes   practice
is a way of remembering your children's favourite lullabies.

The clearest sign of recovery is a shimmer of life   support
me in my old age, allow for a medical   drift
calm in cars at night, sleep is for the   weak
at the knees, comatose in the sheets.

The best flavour of hospital ice cream is raspberry   ripple
outwards in the shape of stolen blood   pressure
below crush depth is enough to make a man   force
majeure. Every gift is perpendicular to cargo for a cult.

I am sorry to have written this, to have wasted your   time
is a construct, a failure to comprehend universal   rule
over me and I'll keep writing. Trust me nobody wants   that
clock is showing the time and date of our deaths again.

Who knew there were so few hours in a day.

RENT-A-PRICK

Isolation is a domestic task we   prove
yourself worthy of solar systems and
endless arrays of space   time
to waste and time to kill my   self
centred and an asshole, then what are you?

I am mundic, this house is falling   apart
of me in every obsession. If I am   made
a cake, baked myself into it, ate my   own
up to our faults or live in this   state
my intentions before I pull the trigger.

Seriously, I taste great as cake, all   cut
up angels and a back catalogue emo   record
yourself hating yourself and play it   back
to back in a barn with a guy your mate
recommended for intensive therapy.

Every time I've considered giving   up
yours, I've never seen a cry for help I didn't   love
me in ways your dad never loved your mum.
We're all skin and bone but some of us have
a reason to power through the hayfever.

BURIAL RITES FOR DISTANT BOATS

Give me an ice cream scoop to the   eyes
so sore it bears repeating that I'm   disappearing
acts are standard fare. When the rain   clouds
my judgement in doing school-runs in   dayglo
of some lost star tracing its arc across   infinity
loose leaf in a strainer, I've gentrified my own hot drinks.

Everything is avoidable with some simple   planning
an escape by jumping into the night, or a   trip
over myself several months into a waking   dream
up a scenario for turning yourself into a   paperchain
mail promising the universe's impending heat   death
defying stunt of tearing my own skin off on TV.

Listen, the soft knock of a hand against a   doorframe
me for my own sabotage. The drugs no longer   work
weekends and slowly towards forever, payslips   filed
my nails down to nothing against a hardwood   floor
me with your love for me, a walking cheap   trick
of loving a man not worth the effort, nor the revelation.

NIGHT SONNETS

by Stuart McPherson

―――――――

Just a poem, not a big project for changing the world.
— Bernadette Mayer, 'Birthday Sonnet for Grace'

NIGHT SONNET #1

Blunt moth tapping at the window
with all empty vessels, a yellow crispness
of spotlights reflected in the frosted glass.
   Evening contemplation is a sad hammer.
No serum for the eyes, last year's presents
have expired, gone off to rattle in the travel
bag. I think about the shadow of summer's
garden, throbbing and uneven, slant foxes,
gnawing little beetles in the curling weeds.
Tinnitus, microwave signals for all lost boys.
   The nighttime torn, unravels from its hem.
I am here for you, with us, for *them*. Within a
mirror stares a man, his pockets full of shells.
   Two grey shotguns under lock & key.

NIGHT SONNET #2

"Don't be forever" she said, although
forever is to be expected and there is
something wondrous about trapping
yourself beneath a gargantuan limb of
night, the frothing of a jagged horse.
Our broken world's nimble fallibility
so very keen to be thumbed through.

Food is rotting in the refrigerator and
heavy trotting is a luddite, an empty
space unable to be seen, but truly felt.
An abstraction incessantly dwelt upon,
same as age creeping in the mangroves,
prickly pears in the desert. The future
watches rabbits thrashing in the snares.

NIGHT SONNET #3

Only the analogous night is full of footprints.
Orange fox running cold amongst the twitch.
Where dusk dulls the tallest men into shapes of baited
hooks, and the weak, the crabby dregs of harbour tide.
How do you bend without drawing breath?

I fall for you, feel the doldrums twist inside the sheets.
Only when each room glows green like a ghost can we
start to reconcile our nakedness. This swell of violence.
Of bent air between twins, the planet Mars........ *please.*

> Take this meagre hand, and in the sky sketch out the
> circumference of two blunt moons. I have come here
> to sleep with a stomach full of wine, this hardening
> of heart. Hard drives corrupt, whittled ends of hair
> snag on shirt buttons fractured into corporate shards.

NIGHT SONNET #4

Chest wrenched torsion crescendos in oblique
limbic hour. Every passing car twists its torque
wrench into overt clicking whilst a collection of
deep holes dig themselves into obese puerility.
This rapidness will be cast out, as gravitational
pulls of gas giants slingshot death orbs into an
arc of quantum calculation. Discard mortalities.
> Cast out distracted connective trivial pursuits.
> Tend instead to all common animals, bicuspid
> resplendence, solar matters soaked inside rich
> tufting of grass. God's woeful pauses coalesce.

The Atlantic meridional overturning circulation
ceases to be a backbone. How salubrious time
spills like an inbox grievance forced to be read.

NIGHT SONNET #5

Whimsical death predicates on how many
feathers disturb sleep. How lowly the hour.
How hurtling from office windows feels on
a soft body sewing up the night with every
conjured murmuration. To conjoin as a birth
twin staring into its own frightened eyes. Of
sheet music, all annotated notes drawn from
poison berries crushed under teeth and hoof.
Almond taste; a cyanide richness readying its
faint desire to live. Ejected by torpedo chute,
not as rabbit, but elegant waxwing wrapping
up its royal feathers, clouds of diamante frost.

Natural beauty cares not, career suicide cares not;
The value of coins clatter loudest in empty pockets.

NIGHT SONNET #6

To transcend is to crush all fang bearing creatures.
And without fear displace from cornice indents the
duplicitous eyes of night floating from summer windows
outward to the fourth dimension. The slumber of rooftop
serenity is the whisper of the moons silver body, its parched
oceans catalytic for crab claws pinched across a ventricle.
Immortality, or the realization that cellular matter will return
to choke the riverbed, that there are new shapes that rise to
pile up the wreckage of the world. Crisp suited, botching and
skulked. They force feed grain to fatten livers as glass eyed
cattle tramp like thunder at the gate, their vapor mimicking
the exhaled freedom of a million clattered candles.
So here ends the day; my body and soul are one.
They flee the shadows cast out from calloused hands.

ANTI-CAPITALIST, ANTI-BASTARD

by Aaron Kent

We are desperate we are fabulous we are Possibly dead.

— Sean Bonney, *Untitled*

THAT ALL OF THIS COULD BE ERASED

Fuck the king,
this world is your own
and the landed gentry aren't on your side.
When all that's left to eat
is the bitter ash of my teeth,
and the tears of lesser poets,
feed them to me.
I want a piece of God,
pan-fried, seared to crispy perfection.
I'm saving my teeth
to tuck into the big guy upstairs.
Who needs five stars on Goodreads
when you've torn the face off God.

TINY THINGS, LIKE AN EGO BURSTING

Gently knocking or rapping,
or carving notches into
the glans as an act of repenting
for every time I've written
a stanza and censored lines.
All these weak poets, like
tone-deaf banjo players,
snapping for a chance to be
tugged off in a forward motion,
laying epigraphs to handshakes,
acknowledgements to banker's kids.
I done it dope, sighted my own
values, and never attended no
ceremony bootlicking lesser men.
Write it and warrant it, never
anything more than growth.

LANDING OUTSIDE WATER

A still life of the core of us as an apple,
night's reluctant race to the bottom
of piss-soaked, still warm, jeans.

I am afraid I have run a marathon in boots
because I don't care for clothes with
no ability to catch me. I need the
comfort of kitchen roll, not the furs

of a drenched thread count. Sorry, she
has learnt this from me, has got
hold of my memories and eaten the
way I raised myself. This whole
weak bladder is admission to a club
of us, soaked in night, looking
for reasons to try again at
another time, another day, another her.

INTRODUCTION TO COMPULSORY SEA SHANTIES

Feeling down the backbeat for too long
swinging down the sad beat insurance
so dope I'm flipping myself for cash,
so rope I'm changing myself for less.
Free range is no space for selling
eggs on the side of the road, edging
to hold a load of held-back two years
and still waiting. We don't ask permission,
we blaze a path and leave the forest for fire wood.
We don't need clearance to poetry journal,
or to learn all the tricks we contour to meet.
We ghost historical fiction as relationship
advice for a subscription monthly fee.

A COLLECTIVE NOUN IS A HOSTILE STATE

The verisimilitude of law is that it too
shatters like glass, like kneecaps, like dreams
caught in the turbine of sleaze.

I have nothing to offer besides cover for
shoplifters, excuses for Fawkes,
pirouettes for smoking ballerinas.

London isn't a pipe dream, it's a clusterfuck
of fences, a haemoglobin swollen
beyond the devolution of a body.

You can't change the system meditating
on a dandelion puff, or thinking yourself worthwhile.
Bettering yourself is astigmatism for the soul.

A RECORDED CONVERSATION WITH AN AWARD-WINNING AUTHOR

In case of fire burn all of them, I told him.
You can, with some practice   see your father's
face in the eyes   of every man you hurt.
You are sorry   and you are forgiven
and you are sorry   and so you lie.
Sooner or later   somebody tells you
we will have to kill our fathers   we will have to eat
our mothers   then write a fuckin' book with all those poems
before dying like   a little house in the breeze.

FRAILTY

by Stuart McPherson

To be a man, without the heaviness it brings
— Andrew McMillan, 'Local Train'

IN THE DUSK OF OUR POST-HONEYMOON ERA

There was a time when our desire coated the back
of a tablespoon   sticky tattoo of ice cream goose bumping
on the sternum   the navel   a notching up of all the rooms
in a house   behind curtains   astral projections transmute
themselves into the cold street   visions of my nakedness
an ear pressed to a keyhole   ghostly vessels just outside
of consciousness   enamored almost   with virtuous noise
the success of sex that blooms into shapes to spill across
a dirty floor   heavy breathing vast and dewy backed
the absolute gloriousness of youth maybe   or something
about time as the drawing in of night   an appearance
of fruit flies around uneaten apples   nonetheless
the quickening of a nervous dog that both of us
labelled ownerless   *I had a dog once* mentioned casually as
course rope taught across our wrists   to signal intertwining
and some things are easier to forget than others
the emergence of shod animal hair becomes harder to pluck
when coated in rheum   lodged in the mucus of a strep throat
heaved from lips once dry with lust and gagged *for now*
by a tail wagging in the garden of a tiny terrace   little lights
blinking in its kitchen   the grey of the sky   its snow
is so much less exciting than it used to be

CLEAR AIR

Always when the rain wraps around this house   the cast iron throat of it   so distant   so vocal in conversance   I observe the crouch of feline shapes under holly trees   the shadowing of the strawberry plants   how all of my back teeth hurt upon waking   *horizontally   vertically*   stuck onto ivory cartilage atoned by two pushed thumbs   how it is that no one really cares anymore?   how lost have I become?   all sleep is just the illusion of rest   *quite useless*   as is my false enjoyment of the stage   a vested interest in amateur dramatics   lying to an audience before obstinately choking on a boiled sweet   cutely coughing for the curtain to fall   *for the intermission*   so happy with my astuteness in the not answering of difficult questions

ELEPHANT CIRCA 1989

Blue grey balloon *in-vibrato* inhabits all empty space
Settles like dust behind a whitewashed dresser   Bedroom
reparations are a spate river whirlpooled with our intimacies
Some better ones   better than *this* at least   like those regularly
delivered to my door   the soles of his feet   or pushed beneath
counters   the hair drooped above temples of children wide
eyed and rippling with adrenaline   the angular contradiction
of epaulettes enjoying the crudeness of a sex-tape   pastille
pinks   blushed pineapple   pina colada   Perfect breasts
poised above the arc of a real man   You'd think that home
was a safe place   but they let it in and up the stairs   It lives
there now   in every room of every house I've ever tried
to fuck in   And when I say *try* I mean cower in its shadow
its four stumped legs   its comorbidities   eyes glowing at the
burial of the one thing meant to hold us both together

SOMEONE LEFT THE DOOR OPEN IN THE WAR ROOM

I'm sorry I let it fall *this snow*   from the rafters of a house
heavy as sleep   to settle on the laundry clasped like brittle
hands dampen the utilities the unopened envelopes all the
things you've done and do I haven't seen that I couldn't stop

myself from sitting still   watched it drift the same as that
time we risked the high road where in panic I dropped the
handbrake to spin the wheels   and now there is a chalking
where you sat your shoulders holding onto its little peaks

a silhouette frozen to the kitchen floor   how snowfall mutes
the footsteps how every inch of pressure crunches into white
malnourished tongues unable to taste our thoughts occluding
in the quietest space floating down the stairs to whip across

our pale skin as flakes soaking into heteronomous lamplit
night   standing up tall hurts watching vapour wrap around
glass is effortless   and in waiting for the pistol there is the
cold sting of every single way I could have made things better

WE ARE STILL HERE DESPITE EVERYTHING

You and this collection of dust   Your hand on my chest
sweeping away the ants lured by an unmopped pulp

Our tongues in the hot tang of night to taste   When all
belongings clatter carelessly on a doorstep then run away so

as to brick themselves inside a new life   leave us to share in
death at the bottom of the stairs   leave it cooling in the bed

its sharp surprise spring loaded with a pulling away of sky
too thin to hold a shadow   We've embraced the cries of

a newborn   deliberately held ourselves underwater   pinched
drowning at the nose   passed air between lips before rising

from the globular silt   We sit upon the rings of Saturn to
watch the folding of an edgeless cloak   to wonder then   why

our hands cannot hold water   or time   or shovel out these
piles of apple pips ground between teeth   All these things

ignored but not *this*   The drift from year to year on a raft
bound by lint woven from our empty pockets   Helpless as

the ripened sun so desperate to outlive its own vapid burning
Same as the tilted earth frightened of its own relentless orbit

DEFICIT

Honestly   even in our best
moments   I think about
the end   so as to

try and live a little
enjoy the privilege
of saltwater erosions or

her shape diving
inside a circumference
of burnt orange

but it's raining now   and the
sand is imprisoned for talking
about yesterday's freedom.

DARLING LET ME DIE IN PEACE

by Aaron Kent

———————

In my dream I apologize to everyone I meet
— Claudia Rankine, 'Don't Let Me Be Lonely'

AN OBITUARY

I have reached out to the obituary writers, and they can't find a valid reason for dying besides being written of and about, or being dismantled by proxy. What good is death if nobody is around to calculate your value and assign it a page number in a clenched fist of a tabloid? I plan to share my little deaths among friends as minor griefs spooled onto mixtapes. Set me up to play somewhere beyond the Mersey, before the Clyde. I think in rivers now, they carry me salty.

FIRE-STARTER

The last human on Earth sitting alone at the foot of a harbour wall has been there since the days of nuclear strikes when the warheads dropped to Earth as starships — now abandoned. They've never eaten, and only drink puddle water, which they purify themselves. Their nails are stained with old, blood-clotted roadkill and each word they form is carefully constructed, so as not to fall on the shoulders of the dead. The Earth — this Earth — has rotted and the Sun is on borrowed time, dwindling to a sickly white ball, a cold and lifeless shopping cart of space. The moon is a skeleton in the sky, it never stops and is already forgotten. Somehow, a gentle hand on the last person's shoulder, and whispered advice, *we're not allowed to take our boots off.*

INCOMPATIBLE AT BEST

Sublime catharsis rendered as an archipelago. O, search me for Atlantis, find your treasures in the way my elbows click at the joints, pop like bubble wrap in the bend and release. Together, through the steam painted glass of our kitchen window, we can watch in feathered menace as two deer, in our garden, shake hands with former president George W. Bush. Death will surely be a sweet release.

A COLLECTION OF DRAMATIC MONOLOGUES ON THE BIG SCREEN

There is a tree in my house, its sap seeping black from my wounds, I cannot breathe when it blooms with its roots in my mouth. When we are reaping we listen for poltergeists and death rattles, for faint knocking in the night, and shards of shattered bark. This tree will kill me, will feed its roots down my throat as cascading notes on a harp. Fair play I say. Fair play to that tree.

POSSUM, DROWNING

It is the most natural thing in the world to leave, so leave and take your sourdough with you. It gives me the shits. I hate being alone more than I hate being with myself, so I'll suffice. The things we make make us sicker and more miserable than we were before, unless we make a mess of things, then we'll have each other to hate. I have made a mess of loving myself, I have made a mess of my sleep hygiene. Is it hygienic to sleep inside a ballistic missile? The night crawls on and a dog dies nearby. I feel bad about it but do not cry, cannot cry, am too much of a scumbag to cry. A man stands in the road with a shotgun. He is not my father, so we tell each other we love each other. What I would do for him to be my father, or two moths dancing in the cold sky. The moon will kill the poets eventually. The snow will turn the dead of December over, gifts for the ever-violent Claus. There are more cops in this world than dreams. There are no accidents, only the end of everything; the first time I ever told a man *no* was when I took his gun from him.

EVENTIDE PRAYER FOR A BASTARD CAPITALIST (OR, HOW TO AVENGE THE DEATH OF SOMEBODY YOU LOVE)

The precision with which a falling cat can kill a family of four depends on the strength of the car's chassis, and whichever planet you live on. Mercury in retrograde resembles the pebbledash promises of a Tory peer, or some bloke raving about the apocalypse at his Daughter's christening. Neither know what they're doing, but both are a stumble and an intrusive thought away from drowning a crying baby. I am done with polluting the shoreline, now I want to obliterate it and its pretty grievances against shipwrecks and Lego blocks. If the water is holy bring it to the boil, bring me to the boil, bring me to the wreckage of a cat imprinting its fallen grace on the bonnet of a car. All it takes is a single feline, and a drunken vicar, to wipe us off the earth, so how do we learn the gentle act of prayer? I am solemn when held in the grip of something so frightful I cannot manifest its malevolence. Cradle us in the corruption of a car bonnet, give mercy to risen apes, all we have left to achieve is bringing the oceans to our doorstep. Pay me no mind, I plan on swimming until my calves seize with cramp.

POST-BREXIT WORKER BLUES

by Stuart McPherson

Like placing a sticking plaster over shotgun wound, we're all wasting our time.

— Geoff Hattersley, 'Motions'

AT THE END OF IT ALL

Sat beside the dry socket of an old
gas fire, I heard a scratching sound.
From the mortarless breast making

its way downwards like the muscles
in a throat, we sat for a while, me and
that tabby cat (now deceased) until it

appeared, a prehistoric arachnid of
giant proportions scuttling from the
thick web and into the cats mouth to

last no more than two chews before
walking off all irksome for wet meat.
I've always hated spiders but tonight

I felt somewhat sad knowing that all
that climbing had led towards a quick
unnoticed death, a lifetime of selling

silk, little dots spreading outwards.
Our accumulations of work and old
age with no recognition whatsoever.

IF ONLY

If only I could breakfast with the dead, break this
crown of eggshell, put a cat amongst the pigeons.

If only I could focus on the trivial pursuits.
Of making plum jam, unravelling yarn, spelunking.

If only I could fix a padlock to my skull. Keep
all the sweet thoughts in, let the obtuse fly away.

If only I could trap all antagonistic beings in a jar.
Dress them with a clowns smile, draw a blue tear.

If only I could see the end as a hole punched in a
map. Allow bitter days to be shaken off like dew.

If only I could walk in nature and be content.
Keep at arm's length the what? the why? the when?

If only I could keep the receipts, her shrunken
clothes, her shoes, close them tightly in my hands.

If only I could stop the rain. Be better at climbing
into galaxies, the stars of Andromeda, Pleiades.

If only I could bend time. Right the wrongs. Wrong
all the rights in need of wronging in the first place.

If only I could find Nicholas Cleménts *other* book.
Show how much energy it *really* takes to boil water.

If only I could end work, abolish all corporate slang
and its utter bastardisation of the human language.

If only I could stop a while. Knock a wedge between
inertia and the force upon a body gradually stripped.

If only I could languish in the joy of dust. Of bed
sheets gentle as ghostly beings brushing the nape.

If only I could speak in tongues. Let the rage of angry
gods flood my ventricles with a hot, acrid liqueur.

If only I could wander the earth as a borderless realm.
Talk wholesomely about how we find our way home.

If only I could sleep amongst the herons. Find safety
with the margin dwellers, swollen flashes of fish.

If only I could cast myself as a sword. Hammer my
bones into sheets of iron, scream into the cool water.

If only as a fool I could learn to love myself. Think not
of how the belly misaligns both trousers and belt.

If only I could enjoy silence, the purity of yoghurt,
the nutritional content of yeast, the snap of ripe melon.

If only I could smother bombs, pluck bullets, lift rubble
into the shape of how a house itself might choose to live.

If only I could count to twenty. If only I could spell. If only I didn't swear. If only I'd left earlier. If only, if only.

SO MANY MEN, SO QUIET THE TOWNS

He hadn't left for months. Sat inside his home
furnished gradually by the working of a forty

year shift, some overtime, thumbing through
that old brochure for Hawaii, San Fran. *Now that*

was a trip he used to say. He didn't like people
eager for the winding up of things. Most of the

time he'd have out all of his Waylon long players.
Have them ready on the deck with a glass of ruby

port and brandy, laughing from his stomach. *Still*
gonna die boy. Whenever I hear country, I think of

him and all that time he did. How he hated Frank
Sinatra, smashed a radio when he heard his voice.

TRUE STORY

I once had a boss who would gather
up the team for every trivial incident.

If you haven't got a positive, find one he said.
That very loathsome evening I wrote my

first and only piece of flash fiction, about
a cohort of cannibal bankers who butchered

and trimmed all new employees, broiled
the brains, feet, and guts, tossed their fried

livers in with the Caesar salad. *Such delicious
meaty lunches*. Wanting opinion, I showed it

to my friends, the general consensus that it
was way too violent, almost unnecessarily so.

FROM DISPATCH TO SUBURBIA

Fucking fuck knows he said, in verbatim.
My friend had come to see about batteries
for his camera on my appraisal that this
warehouse had everything from diode to
dimmer switch. A place he'd worked his
whole life, even met his true love, the girl
whose mother asked me to call her to talk
her out of it. I see them from time to time,
now husband and wife. Our children attend
the same school. I never could tell if he was
happy. He still looks the same, wears that
same green bomber jacket, although now
it has a grey panel stitched across the back.

GREAT BRITAIN

The litter peppered the roadside.
Not quite a drift, but surprising as
snow when operatic in its entrance.

The grey sky sucked on its butt-end.
The grass lolled, dark, thick green,
unkempt as hair hidden under hat.

Even from the air the sea stunk like
a shithouse and all public transport
melted from the lightest kiss of rain.

The doctors ghosted their patients.
The ghosts of patients ghosted the
politicians in their holiday homes.

Politicians ghosted themselves now
unable to be classified as humanoid,
warped wooden slat, or iron hobnail.

The children licked the rust from
the railings. Salt, essential minerals,
record funding less miscalculation.

A song produced under frayed flag.
The droll anthem of a wrung-necked
chicken limping home to roost.

ALL ENGLISH WANK

by Aaron Kent

I could not account for myself
— Fran Lock, White / Other

ONCE MORE WITH A BODY COUNT

alumni is just a fancy word for intubation for breaking your mother's heart with debt she was too poor for bankruptcy i am working through the night like i am picking through the debris of a hot air balloon accident's incessant glimmer of a call to darkness this gospel is a nightly derangement for routines i've found book-time for okay here's the light as phosphorescent what do you mean the momentum of our choices are divisible by three you've never made it through a poem this dark so why start now when you could empty the dishwasher and slowly roast in the outside world like a weatherman gone rogue i hate how much i love my knees the residue of line-caught salmon hums inside us like we're all stardust or the remnants of a bear mowing down passengers in an eighty nine chevy mow me over with your desperate love play me as we dance under a shower of gasoline fuck it you've burnt us all and now we're counting pen lids and praying to gods made of clam shells

TWO TRUTHS AND A LIE, BUT THEY'RE ALL TRUE

i don't know how much longer you expect me to live but there are ghosts in these walls and goddammit i'll join them if i can if i know what's good for me i'll love you until it hurts to breathe and then some i owe you the grace of my final words i couldn't bring myself to cry for you it's the only thing i learnt from my dad and i'll be cold in the ground before i give him the satisfaction you are the sleeper train at midnight steadfast in static momentum a small mercy in amongst the misery my favourite thing and more let's share photographs of dogs arguing over a ball i'm not sure i know what it's like to love something so insignificant with such force but i think with enough bandages i might learn how to love myself yet

SORRY, MY LOVE

intravenous drip me holy come and swear i do the things men do when they hide under covers tell me the world has space for new mercies like we share space for the night's dense gravity you are never nearer than i can promise to be we are always just so from getting enough for a deposit enough for me to make a home if i am to be manly and dense i shall bring you bread to break with every meal and bones i broke with every KILL ME SOFTLY ENOUGH THAT THE FLESH I LEAVE BEHIND MAY MUTATE INTO FOOD FOR LIVE CULTURES OR TONIC for a hungry caterpillar a chrysalis can make space exist for family photos but you're always just starting again there is no do-over for the immaculate preening of a face mask at midnight christ kill me now save me the small task of applying pressure to a wound and caring enough to tear my shirt to shreds

WHILE POPPING THE FILM ON A READY MEAL I CONSIDER TURNING THE KNIFE ON MYSELF

when you must carve your brain from its placeholder descale your hands first bring the mechanics of your skeleton to a boil stand lofty above it all views from the top of babel are only significant to those climbing it and those in the polished concrete above the rest of us are knee deep in brain jelly the consistency of dog meat's peculiar housing

CROMULENT CREAMPIE

if god were real a sizeable portion of the population would accuse him of being in kahoots with big pharma the big g paid off by moneymen to push prayer anything to help paranoid minds gnosh each other off with tales of spiritual genocide or david icke declaring in the waffle of a man knee deep in his own lunacy that he knows of hush money paid for jesus' laptop nobody actually believes in conspiracies they merely believe in the sum total of their own issue with authority figures at least have the tenacity to admit the world is round and you just can't stand the sight of your kids pissing in a university urinal if god were real the tories would prostrate themselves in front of him with a finger on the pulse of their prostate in hopes the big guy would consider buying an abandoned building to house a fake broadband company anything to increase the flow of money funnelled directly into their velveted assholes the only thing stopping the second coming is figuring out how many kids boris johnson got from the first

LAZARUS' LEFT BOLLOCK

these bruises like sediment to the live supreme these hands carpenters for their own gristle and snares their own inevitable slide into madness and surrounding dominions every church has a reason for fitting miniscule pews but i don't understand their obsession for madness nor their vehicle for violence the first time my dad died he did so threatening his dissolution with a noose every subsequent time he vanished a little further from view until he swung back round to resurrection i want to punch a man with these wood-stained hands i want to watch me bleed i want to demolish myself blow by blow petty cut by paper cut.

ADOLESENCE IS A BITTER PILL SWALLOWED TWICE

by Stuart McPherson

———————

Now, in the dark, he dreams.

– Kim Addonizio, 'Ever After: A Paradelle'

NOT ALL TEENAGE BEDROOMS ARE THE SAME.

Replay this June night like a rock song. Lavish in
the drone of distant traffic, hamstrings sunken into
uncomfortable hulks of stained mattress rattling
its metal innards, its threat of wounded skin. I know
that I am nothing, just some offcuts clattering in a bag
so unwanted by the discontent sat downstairs with all
their brooding bodies. What's eating them is eating me too
and I think about sex like a toothache, that time I sat
across from her, how the wallpaper was a beige floral
shroud hanging our embarrassment across the innards
of a cube. I love this music, how it matches with the dusk.
This cassette is chewed, on the edge of breaking and
I guess I had to hopscotch through it all just to live.
The humming of a bee, the birds rampant in the cold
blue dawn. The future is pushed into my eyes by the tinnitus of
pornography vibrating in its black, vacuous box.
I love the foolish lust of this season, the gentle
resting of my chin, hands on windowsill gazing up
at the stars, that singular cloud. Everything is inconvenient.
Everywhere is littered with the seedy failure of man.

ADOLESCENT NOSTALGIA IS NEVER A ONE TRICK PONY

I used to wait for them, the outcasts.
My age group full of wholesome shapes,
and me, blurring at the edges unable to be
seen without spectrometer.
And when *they* came *I became*,
forever on the fringes where they hid me
in their hearts. We sang along
to the Subhumans and did hot knives
and they kept me safer than a family home.
We screamed the words *'from birth, to school, to work,
to death, from the cradle to the grave,'* punched
all grey smoke from the air and I wonder
what I would have become without them.
Without the music and delinquency to show me
right from wrong.

OVERDRAMATIC HALLOWEEN SEX POEM

Sex is awkward as the innards of a pumpkin,
don't you think?

Glossy and alluring. An excitement when revealed
but cooling to the touch.

Until in boredom it sits there all fibrous, decapitated,
oozing with pips. The body it was scooped from

wears an ugly face, a happy face, depending
on perspective, on how you see it.

Pointed teeth, an acute triangular nose
so as to not take itself *too* seriously.

A pumpkin is as real it gets in terms of where the
brain sits, but the stomach and the heart are lost.

Ill-considered like Carpenter's *Halloween*.
All those teenagers in a throbbing frenzy to fuck.

All those lanterns forced to watch from bedside tables,
from front porches under bedroom windows.

And Michael Myers with towering guilt punishes all.
With anxiety and fear like a wet, eternal grave.

How do we make peace with the season?
How do you extract the grief from all hallowed souls?

Ironic that a fruit grown in seclusion must be
romanced by the sun; the petite, delicate rain.

To then light up so briefly in the dark, to climax in
the dead of night, only to be switched off,

discarded, is programmed to decompose,
leak oily fluid so that no one then wants to look or feel.

It's all so brief, and omnipresent.
And no one tells you how to carve.

How to peel back the lid. They tell you though,
how not to make a mess, clean up, be hygienic.

But there is always *something* left behind.
A seed, a lurid orange stain.

Maybe it's because I was exposed to
horror as a kid.

I turned out ok, I guess.
I take a few pills now and then, who doesn't?

Although the memory of her appears,
all naked in the lowlights of that specific failure.

The disappointment in her voice.
About sex not being the same as portrayed on film.

And as my jeans stretch the question against my toes,
I think that somehow, *it always is.*

THE PUNK'S PICNIC WAS INSANE

I don't want you to know that I'm safe,
I want you to feel instead like a father should,
see the police nervous and agitated at
our presence, the piss yellow
afternoon getting hotter and hotter.
I want you to see the people I'm with,
that they are good people, look after me,
buy me alcohol and would never let me
huff from that bag of brown toffee, let alone
allow it to touch my lips. You said you drove
around the city looking for me, reptilian tears
welling in your vertical slits. I know I said I'd be
there to sit by myself whilst you continued
with your middle-class enterprise, that
ridiculous book on astral projection,
or digging your way towards both capitalism
and communism at the same time, but guess what,
it was deliberate. I just wanted you to know
that I was having the time of my fucking life.

WITHOUT FAILSAFES

You spike your hair with soap, shape it to a point.
Primary colours dance between the ripples of a boy
skipped across a lake. Suddenly you're a man, or the
outline of one embossed in heaps of rattling shale.

Being a man is hard when you haven't yet been a boy.
You are scared to fight, but don't think before kicking
the headlights of a bouncers truck. Here are the arms
of the woman who took your virginity, outstretched.

You don't talk about sex, you fear it, and despite all the
the bragging rights, you never said a *thing*. This anxiety
suit is a jackhammer and that girl you never slept with
was cheating on you too. Guilt sinks its ropes of oily

slick innards to the bottom with the rays and moray eels
and you have wild friends and by the time others catch
up, you are wilder still and they see something in your
eyes like the body of a hitchhiker crouched between two

parked cars. How do you spell 'gradually'? How do you
write the introduction to a cold world? You are here and
one day you might come clean, but until then fulfil all the
prophecies, hail brutalism, and to failure, *yeah, fuck you too.*

RELIEF

The young never see their beginnings.
Of crisp chinese apples sweet enough to blow
giddiness through the orchard of themselves.
They smell the green leather seats, the tobacco,
hear the laughter of guardian angels, a house band
out of time and know that *this is how we do it.*
At night they dizzy themselves. That winter air,
the way it smells so thick. Like sugared spearmint
propping up the stars. There's a romance in the drinking
so contagious for young bodies. But the young never see
the fault lines filling up with grain, the liquid lapping
at the edge until in torsion the land pulls itself apart,
buildings shake, melting like chocolate in the sun and
the moon becomes a malt froth surging with fizz.
Maybe our grandparents tried to tell us, but in the hour
of need they slept too long and there is a beautiful rainbow
arcing across the wardrobes holding all unworn clothes.
The young never see their beginnings, or know,
that the sound of splitting open a pine door holds the same
frequency as starting a new life, although there it crawls,
twitching inside our violent dreams.
Of course, there are options. There is a love of ignorance too,
especially when the young realise that their destiny,
is to never actually awake up at all.

EPHEMERAL MATERIAL INCIDENT

by Aaron Kent

An infinitude of Octopus eyes
— Stuart McPherson, 'Gasp Reflex'

TO DISAPPEAR. TO FALL ASLEEP

The noise of a hammer on a footstep.
    The waning of the bed of a nail. It follows

that I press abdominal to flesh, press my
    stem to the interference of our sleeping

gristle. How to peel the sunburn from
    an apple. How to slaughter a windowpane

for eventide. A single magpie puncturing
    car tyres, a nest shedding itself. Glass

breaking in all directions, a fever of shards
    alighting with conditions. Outwards and

towards the sea with a fear of maritime lore.
    Creating new forgeries, alarms clocks

for invisible dawns. Of reprehensible longitude.
    Of another morning left to its own devices.

MISSION ANALYSES: RHODEDENDRON

by Stuart McPherson

In hindsight, there's too many poems that exist to be poems, too many PE teachers tensing their chests for meagre applause
— Aaron Kent, 'Imagine what he could've done if he used his MAXIMUM HEADROOM'

A KAPUŐRÖK MEGSZŰNÉSE / HERLIN-BAMLET PART II

I'm sorry, but a fox is better
at public relations and solar
architecture than the shadow
of a comet engulfed in true
meanings of autumnal bonfires.

If I wanted to know about
the phosphorescence of oysters
sipped inside resplendent ballrooms,
I would lavish in the nepotistic
grandeur of their empty shells.

All silent battalions loosen
inside the nest of a heron more
concerned with the arrival of snow.
The potential for beaks to fracture
oceanic maps of a bloodline.

Ordinary sleep is avoidant of
nuclear weapons, and my teeth
are longer than any young pipsqueak
wanting to be outlived. I apologize,
Borbély, but the hierarchies can

only be smashed by the sacrifice
of a coffin rolled across a minefield.
The sniping of all expensive tyres
to burst our children's headaches
foraged from dead tradition.

SHARE OUT YOUR UNREST

www.ingramcontent.com/pod-product-compliance
Lightning Source LLC
Chambersburg PA
CBHW022114090426
42743CB00008B/846